The Ducky

D C Jackson's first full-length play, *The Wall*, won the Best Ensemble at the 2007–8 Critics' Awards for Theatre in Scotland and was shortlisted for the Saltire Society/Royal Mail Scottish First Book of the Year Award. He has had short plays produced by Oran Mor (*Matinee Idle, Drawing Bored, Out on the Wing*), the Arches Theatre Company (*Hello,* part of *Spend a Penny*) and Borderline Theatre Company (*Chib!*). He is working on new plays for BBC Radio 4, the National Theatre of Scotland and the Royal Court, and was the Pearson Writer in Residence at the Royal Court for 2008.

D C JACKSON

The Ducky

faber and faber

First published in Great Britain in 2009
by Faber and Faber Limited
74–77 Great Russell Street, London WC1B 3DA

Typeset by Country Setting, Kingsdown, Kent CT14 8ES
Printed in England by CPI Bookmarque, Croydon, Surrey

A CIP record for this book
is available from the British Library

ISBN 978-0-571-25259-6

2 4 6 8 10 9 7 5 3 1

Acknowledgements

I mainly wrote this play while imposing on the hospitality of Arash and Kate, Hermeet, Emma Justice, the Royal Court Theatre and, briefly but memorably, the Stemplowski family.

Thanks are due to Liz Lochhead, Lyndsey Turner, Jemima Levick, Becky Minto, Finn Den Hertog, Sally Reid, Johnny Austin, Andrew Milne, Lisa Foster and Jacqueline, Ben and Edward as well as all the staff of Borderline Theatre Company. I am exceptionally grateful to Dinah Wood, Steve King and everyone at Faber for their continued support.

This one goes out to all my dead homies – Gran and Papa, Granny Jackson, Aunt Alice and Neera.

D C Jackson, Glasgow, April 2009

The Ducky was commissioned and produced by
Borderline Theatre Company, Ayr, and first performed
at the Palace Theatre, Kilmarnock on 2 May 2009.
The cast was as follows:

Michelle Hannah Donaldson
Rab Finn den Hertog
Norma Sally Reid
Trevor Alan Tripney
Cooney Jonathan Holt

Director Jemima Levick
Designer Becky Minto
Lighting Designer Jeanine Davies
Stage Manager Rob Armstrong
Wardrobe Supervisor Jennie Loof
Fight Direction David Goodall
Producer Eddie Jackson

THE DUCKY

Setting

'The Ducky' is a septic swimming hole on the outskirts of the small Ayrshire town of Stewarton. High banks on either side of the still pool are dotted with gorse bushes. A long-abandoned pair of pants hangs from one of the bushes. Train tracks run close by – going in one direction to Glasgow and in the other Kilmarnock.

The stage rises to a ridge at the back, twelve feet beneath which (unseen) is the water.

Act One

PROLOGUE

The Friday coming.
  Lights.
  *Rab McGuire is centre stage. He is dressed for a
funeral in a black suit and tie. He is soaking wet because
he has been swimming in the Ducky fully clothed. His
white shirt is muddy and his shoes leak water. He is
exhausted. As soon as we see him he lets out the cry:*

Rab Fucking-~~cunting~~-shitty-bastard-arsehole-pissflaps-
spunkpot-dirty-motherfucking-fannyrag-bums-tits-turd-
arse-fuck!

  Lights.

SCENE ONE

Friday. August 2007 – the sunny week. The Ducky.
  *Trevor McGuire is seventeen. He has bright red hair,
jug ears and the physique of a long-term coma victim.
He is practising his kung fu. Self-taught, he is both a bad
student and a terrible teacher. He conducts a dialogue
with himself, enthusiastically mimicking the accents in
dubbed Chinese films.*

Trevor 'You have the style of a ninja.'
  'I know every style.'
  'Do you know the style of the Bullfrog? The Mad
Dog? The Violent Frog?'

  *Neil Cooney is a sixteen-year-old lout. He runs onstage
dressed to swim. He shouts as he runs:.*

3

Cooney FUCK OFF! GET OUT OF THE WAY, TREVOR, YOU BIG GINGER TAMPON! AND STOP SNIFFING ROUND MY BIRD!

He runs past Trevor and jumps off the bank into the Ducky below.
Sound of a splash.
Trevor begins his kung fu again.

Trevor 'A hero chooses his battles.'

Norma Gordon enters. She is sixteen.

Norma God, Trevor.

Trevor What?

Norma You knew I was coming up the Ducky.

Trevor So?

Norma So? What are you doing here?

Trevor Why should I not be, Norma?

Norma I'm not going to be doing anything.

Trevor Okay.

Norma I'm just going to sit for a bit. And think. Quietly.

Trevor Uh-huh.

Norma On my own.

Trevor does not leave.

God, Trevor. You're so annoying.
  I just saw you twenty minutes ago. You must of run from down the street. I mean. Stalked. What? What is that, Trevor?

Trevor Nothing. I just . . .

Norma Gonnae just stop . . . you're freaking me out.

Trevor It's a free country.

Norma And I should be free to be on my own if I want.

Trevor I'm not doing anything.

Norma . . . without getting bugged by you.

Trevor I'm not bugging you.

Norma You are but. You are bugging me.

Trevor I didn't mean to.

Norma God. I wish you would just leave me alone. You're always there. Every time I turn around, there you are.

Trevor I thought we were friends.

Norma Arrrrrgh . . . We are. We're *just* friends, Trevor.

Trevor I'm just being friendly.

Norma Too friendly.

Trevor Fine.

He still does not leave.

Norma Really? Really, Trevor? You're just going to stand there?

Trevor Maybe.

Norma Oh for God's sake, Trevor. This isn't right. You're not right.

Trevor Fine then. I'm going. I was here first *but.*

He exits. Norma watches him go. then looks over the edge of the bank into the Ducky.

Norma Hiya, Neil.

Sound of a wolf-whistle from the Ducky.
  Norma watches Cooney swim.
  Michelle Montgommery enters. At eighteen, her
childhood goth look is now drifting into indie.

Michelle Hi, Norma.

Norma No way – Michelle! How's Barassie?

Michelle I don't live in Barassie any more – I'm at uni.

Norma Glasgow or Strathclyde?

Michelle Caledonian.

Norma Oh . . .
  Well . . .
  At least it's in Glasgow. At least you're not at Paisley.

Michelle Yeh.

Norma I heard about your great-gran, Michelle. I'm
sorry. I really liked Minnie. *Like*. Like. Sorry.

Michelle It's fine.

Norma How is she?

Michelle Yellow.

Norma God. That's a sin. Is she allowed visitors?

Michelle Yeh.

Norma Would it be alright if I went in and saw her?

Michelle I suppose . . . I wouldn't. Really.

Norma Oh.

  Silence.

So is that how you're back then?

Michelle Yeh. Sort of. I mean, it's the summer holidays
and I don't really . . . I mean . . . yes.

Norma Where you staying?

6

Michelle Corsehillbank Street.

Norma Minnie's house?

Michelle Yeh. I'm looking after Sebastian.

Norma Aww . . . wee Sebastian. How is he?

Michelle She.

Norma What?

Michelle She. Sebastian's a girl. Minnie calls all her cats Sebastian.
She bought an engraved collar in the fifties.

Norma How is she then?

Michelle She's not well either. I'm taking her to the vet's.

Norma God. Sometimes they say that happens, don't they? In sympathy. Psychically. Like a phantom pregnancy, I mean. Not like that really. I mean. Like . . . I don't know. Pets.
Are your mum and . . . em . . . your . . . her . . . Em. Her . . .

Michelle Her girlfriend. You can say it.

Norma Bit weird calling old Alice from the Health Food Shop a girlfriend, but. She's pretty old.

Michelle Her partner then. If you prefer.

Norma Then they sound like detectives. Alice and June – Organic Detectives – Macrobiotic Investigators. Sorry. Aye, your mum and Alice, her partner, here too?

Michelle No. They're away at a spa for a few days.

Norma A Spar?

Michelle Yeh. They need some time away together. They haven't really been getting on.

7

Norma Oh. How a Spar?

Michelle I don't know. They wanted time alone together
. . . to talk. Get treatments. Massages. That kind of thing.

Norma At a Spar? They don't even have a decent selection
ready meals.

Michelle What?

Norma A Spar. Isnae even a real supermarket. How are
they doing massages now?

Michelle Not a Spar. A *spa*.

Norma Oh right. A spa. Right. *Spa*.
    So they've just left you to look after Sebastian and
look in to Minnie on your own?

Michelle I said I would. It's fine. I don't mind. I mean,
my mum's been in to the hospital twice a day every day
for months. From Barassie. They both have. I mean. I
wanted to come back anyway. I missed . . . Anyway. So.

Norma Why? If I ever left Stewarton I would never come
back. Stewarton is a total shit tip.

Michelle It isn't that bad.

Norma Yes it is. Have you forgotten? It's a cowp. At
least Barassie has the shore.

Michelle The shore's shite.

Norma Yeh.

    Pause.

Michelle How's your brother?

Norma He's your boyfriend.

Michelle I know.

Norma Well, don't you?

Michelle What?

Norma Know.

Michelle I got an email last week.

Norma I think he's in Thailand now.

Michelle Good for him. *pause.*

Norma He isnae a sex tourist.

Michelle No. I know. Travelling. I know.

Norma Have you told him about Minnie?

Michelle I didn't . . . I didn't want to . . . You know. By email. Or on his Facebook wall. I mean.

Norma Yeh.

Michelle I mean, I didn't want him to think I was asking him to come back . . . I'm not. It's fine. I'm fine. Fine. Anyway . . . what else?

Norma How do you mean?

Michelle Any other news?

Norma Em. I don't know – it's Stewarton. Oh! You know Gonk?

Michelle Yeh.

Norma He's lost a ball.

Michelle How do you mean, 'lost a ball'?

Norma A testicle ball.

Michelle No way!

Norma Aye. God's honest, Michelle. He was climbing up a tree in Andy Bell's garden and he was wearing these wee shorts and then he fell out.

Michelle How does that mean he's lost a ball?

Norma His bag / tore on a branch.

Michelle His bag?

Norma His ball bag, and then one came out and Andy Bell's dog ate it.

Michelle That's not true.

Norma It is. Now he's got a glass ball.

Michelle A glass ball?

Norma Like a glass eye.
  But I think it's silicone. Like a boob. It's seriously aw round my work.

Michelle Where do you work?

Norma Krazy Kutz.

Michelle Which one? With a C or a K?

Norma Original. Krazy Kutz wi' a K.

Michelle How long have you worked there?

Norma A while.

Michelle Is it good?

Norma It's fine.

Michelle You full-time?

Norma Yeh. I'm not a hairdresser or anything but.

Michelle You a trainee?

Norma I'm a sweeper.

Michelle Can you become a trainee there though?

Norma Suppose. If I wanted.

Michelle Do you not want to?

Norma I don't really like touching aw they folks' heads. You should see some of the clatty articles we get in. An' I worry about the chemicals.

Michelle At least it's a trade, or a skill, or you know, something. Better than a degree.

Norma There's already a trainee on the now.

Michelle Who?

Norma Rochelle McManus.

Michelle Oh . . .

Norma Yeh.

Michelle So what are you going to do?

Norma Do you know? I have literally no idea.

Michelle You could do anything.

Norma . . . Anything but sweeping.

Michelle The possibilities are endless . . . You've got the world at your feet.

Norma Yeh. World at my feet.

She looks down.

It is though. Isn't it? At all our feet, all the time. So, you know, what does that even mean?

Michelle looks down too.

Yeh . . . anyway. I need to get off. I'm going to Kilmaurs.

Michelle Why?

Norma You kidding? Kilmaurs? It's jumping.

Michelle Oh. Okay. See you round, Norma.

Norma And don't worry, Michelle. He'll be back before you know it.

She exits. Michelle continues looking at the world at her feet. Rab enters. Nineteen years old, he is dressed like a 1980s soccer casual.

Rab Good afternoon, my dear.

Michelle I'm sorry?

Rab It's me.

Michelle . . .

Rab Rab. Rab McGuire. Dashing, devil-may-care Rab McGuire.

Michelle Rab? My God. You look . . .

Rab Hot aye? Aye. Hot.

He inspects himself.

I'm pretty hot.

Michelle You look –

Rab Sexy? Aye, ahm sexy.

Michelle Different.

Rab Aye, time makes fools of us all. How's Barry?

Michelle Travelling.

Rab Aye? Good for him. You'll be looking a long time if you want to find yourself in Ayrshire.

Michelle Yeh.

Rab Your gran awright?

Michelle gives him a look.

Aye – has she no' got leukaemia or something?

Michelle How did you –

Rab I was in the Co-op for ginger. Heard about your gran, Lewis Khan's engagement and Willie Wilson's sex change.

Michelle Willie Wilson has had a sex change?

Rab Nah it turns out he hasnae. I think he's just grown his hair long . . .

Michelle Well, my great-gran does have cancer.

Rab That's shite.

Michelle Yeh.

Rab Barry coming back?

Michelle No. It's fine.

Rab . . . Your maw still a lesbian?

Michelle Yeh.

Rab Cool. You seen my wee brother?

Michelle What does he look like?

Rab Ginger. I got the looks. And the brains. But he got the big bedroom so, you know, swings and roundabouts . . .
      Family, eh? Murder.

Michelle Yeh.

Rab looks around.

Rab Stewarton ay? Who needs to travel the world?

Michelle Yeh.

Pause.

Stewarton to Barassie.

Rab What?

Michelle Glasgow to Edinburgh. Maybe even Aberdeen. Or an Island. Like Arran. That's long distance.

Rab I don't –

Michelle And because sixteen miles is fine, six thousand is? Really? What is that?

Barry's away, what? Getting stoned on a beach at some full-moon party? Getting a henna tattoo and his hair braided? Talking to private-school girls in flip-flops?

And I'm up the Ducky with Rab McGuire . . . Fuck their flip-flops.

Rab I can't help but feel the inference there, Michelle – correct me if I've picked you up wrong, the inference you were making was that enjoying a relaxing 'hing aboot wi' me at East Ayrshire's most salubrious natural spring is in some way inferior to living it up in tropical locales.

She does not reply.

Well. That's just offensive.
Balmy climate?

He licks his finger and holds it to the wind.

Check.
Aquamarine water?

He looks over and inspects the Ducky.

Check.
Beautiful people?

He looks first himself and then Michelle up and down.

Check.
Aw you need is a fruity drink and you're away.
No?
Fair enough.
How you liking uni, anyway?

Michelle Not.

Rab How?

Michelle It's shit.

Rab Right.

Michelle What's the point?

Rab Better yourself, intit?

Michelle At Glasgow Calley? Who betters themself at Glasgow Calley?

Rab Emm . . .

Michelle University is meant to be different. Isn't it? That's the whole point.

Rab Different to what?

Michelle School.

Rab Ha! It is just school, Michelle. University, college, work – it's all just school. That's aw there is. A bunch of dicks being dicks to you.
And repeat . . .

Michelle I know.

Rab And repeat.

Michelle I know. I know that. Lectures and classes and canteens. But everything . . . fundamental is meant to change, isn't it?

Rab How do you mean?

Michelle Uni's where you break out of your chrysalis.

Rab How?

Michelle I don't know. Meet like minds. Have your horizons broadened. New . . . fun . . . Everything, everything is meant to change. But it doesn't, does it?

Same people, same pubs, same Sauchiehall Street, same trains and same tube, same Top Shop . . . same *everything*. Same me. Same same same.

Nothing changed. Nothing's different. It's all just the same.

Rab Half your luck. Cambridge is like going tae uni on the fucking moon, man. Wie a bunch of Martians.

Michelle See, that's what I mean, that must be brilliant. Cambridge. That's going to uni. That's life-changing.

Rab Hmph.

Michelle It's amazing, Rab. What an amazing opportunity.

Rab Aye well. Here's the thing about amazing opportunities – they're shite.

Michelle Shite?

Rab Shite. I'm an iconoclast.
There's me, Scouse Chris, three Indian boys and Pepe the Mexican bandito – he's a Pinochet Scholar. Every other wan of them is a plastic-replicant-toff-jockey at my college.
I know it seems like I've got it made, but it isnae . . . I mean . . . it's . . .
The thing about Cambridge is . . .

Trevor enters.

Here he is. The man himself. Awright, wee broseph.

Trevor Hi, Rab.

Michelle Hi – Trevor? I'm Mich—

Trevor I know you are. Who you are. I know who you are. I know that.

Michelle Okay . . .

Trevor Because you go out with Barry – Norma's brother Barry. Barry Gordon. From Standalane.

Michelle I should get going . . .

Rab No. You don't have to. I mean . . .

Michelle Yeh. Leave you boys to catch up.

Rab Okay. Right.
I'll see you around then.

Trevor Bye, Michelle Montgommery. Goodbye.

Michelle Bye, Trevor. Bye.

She exits.

Rab So . . .

Trevor So?

Rab So . . .

Trevor So?

Rab So . . .

Trevor So?

Rab What's the news?

Trevor Em. I dunno. They're doubling the train track. So that they can, em, double the trains.

Rab Aye? You cannae halt progress. Double the trains. Make Stewarton twice as good ay?

Trevor Still Stewarton but.

Rab Yeh.

Trevor Yeh.

Rab Where you thinking about for uni?

Trevor Art school.

Rab Art school aye? Dad'll love that.

Trevor I was thinking. I was thinking about Falmouth. Do a foundation first.

Rab Falmouth? Where the fuck's Falmouth?

Trevor Far'est away from Stewarton.

Rab Stewarton is a hole, right, no one's denying that, but once you're away you're away. Doesnae matter if it's Moscow or Moscow. [*The second Moscow is a village in Ayrshire; it is pronounced Moss Cow.*]

Silence.

Trevor You home for the whole summer?

Rab I expect so. Play it by ear. I was thinking about maybe starting karate while I'm here. Or kung fu. Or Pilates. Is that one? No.

Trevor Why?

Rab Just took a notion.

Trevor Okay . . .

Rab Would you come with me? I know you watch the films and that and I thought –

Trevor You are transparent. Mum's idea?

Rab I just thought it would be good. To hang wi' my wee bro.

Trevor I'm a lover not a fighter.

Rab Trevor. Mum and Dad are . . . worried.

Trevor The paedophiles in Dunlop or the mobile-phone mast?

Rab What happened to your gutties?

Trevor Everyone gets bullied.

Rab Bullied? You're seventeen.

Trevor So?

Rab Bullying is like binge drinking. It disnae really exist. Middle-class fandannery. ~~Just cos they make a HEBS advert doesnae make it so.~~ Who's been gieing you shit?

Trevor Who doesn't? I'm a big ginger dick-target.
The bams, the maddies, the goths . . .
The Venture Scouts . . .
The school band . . . Neil Cooney.

Rab The Venture Scouts? The Venture Scouts? They're a bunch of trainee paedos. And the school band? Fuck sake, man. Only wee emo gaydoughs get bullied. You're my wee brother – I'm Rab McGuire.

Trevor See where the Q8 used to be?

Rab Aye.

Trevor And the bakery?

Rab Aye but –

Trevor It's aw flats now but intit?

Rab Wanker flats uh huh . . .

Trevor And see the Safeway's a Somerfield?

Rab Aye but –

Trevor Everything changes.

Rab I'm still one hundred per cent bam. The tracksuit remains the same.

Trevor You're not wearing a tracksuit.

Rab It's metaphorical.

Trevor And this is the last summer folk'll go swimming in the Ducky.

Rab How?

Trevor They're going to build a swimming pool.

Rab No they're no'.

Trevor Yes they are.

Rab No they're no'. East Ayrshire propaganda. They're always going to build a swimming pool in Stewarton, always. They never dae but dae they? They just use the money to put in more CCTV cameras. Folk'll be swimming in Neilson Baths until the end of time.

Cooney enters.

Cooney I thought I told you to fuck off, Trevor, you squirrel rapist? Right, get your fucking shoes off, they're going in the Ducky.

Rab Excuse me?

Cooney You too, moonface, get your shoes off for Cooney.

Rab Are you joking?

Trevor starts to take his shoes off.

What are you doing? Don't take your shoes off.

Cooney Who are you, mate?

Rab I'm Rab McGuire.

Cooney That supposed to mean something?

Rab It means you need to walk away.

Cooney What are you going to do? You're about as hard as Pele's wang, man.

Trevor Please. Let's just go, Rab.

Rab We're going nowhere.

Trevor Come on. Please?

Cooney Listen to your brother, man.

Rab squares up to Cooney, his mood suddenly, violently switching.

Rab If you ever. *Ever.* Even *go near* my brother again I will fucking destroy you.
Got it? Got it?
Got it?

Cooney Aye.

Rab Good.

Rab walks away. Trevor trots after him.

Cooney Aye, you better walk away . . . before I put a cap in yo ass.

Rab A cap in my ass?

Rab laughs.

A cap in my ass?

He shakes his head in baffled amusement as he exits.

You're funny.

Cooney is alone.

Cooney Dick.

Sound of a train passing by. ✳ sfx
                                 lights down

21

lights up

SCENE TWO

Saturday.
    Norma is at the Ducky. She has a large bottle of Diet Irn Bru which she is attempting to drain. Trevor enters, excitedly clutching a comic he has drawn himself.

Trevor I've drawn a comic.

Norma Okay . . .

Trevor It's called 'Gimp Man vs Super Ninja'.

Norma Okay.

Trevor Because I noticed . . . there's just kind of like, a fine line, between a gimp and a ninja. Look.

    He offers it to her.

Norma Yeh, it looks really good, Trevor. Listen, I need to go.

Trevor It's for you. I drew it for you.

Norma Em. Thanks.

    She takes it reluctantly.

Trevor Norma. I. Em.
    You know. Em. Norma. I mean. I'm not. I wanted to –

Norma Em. Thanks, Trevor, I'll read it at home. I need to jazz just now.

    She flees with 'Gimp Man vs Super Ninja'. Trevor is alone.

Trevor Norma. I really like you. When I'm with you, and you're nice to me, even sometimes when you're not, everything's better.

22

I think we're a bit the same and no one else is even a bit like me and that's lonely and maybe you're the same way and maybe we could . . .

He shakily adopts the pose of the praying mantis.

SCENE THREE

Saturday, continued.
    Lights up on Cooney. Norma enters, sees Cooney.

Norma Hiya.

Cooney Awright.

Norma Trevor McGuire not here?

Cooney Naw.

Norma Thank God. I was here earlier and he was pure creeping me out.

Cooney Aye? Twonk man. I'll get him telt.

Norma Don't. It's fine. He's harmless. I'm glad you're here. I need to speak to you.

Cooney Aye?

She sits down. Long silence.

Norma Do you ever think about the future, Cooney?

Cooney Like spaceships and shit?

Norma No, I mean like your future. What's in your future.

Cooney Spaceships and hoverboards and lasers. And sexy alien birds wi' pointy boobs.

Norma Seriously. What your life is going to be like.

23

Cooney I suppose. Naw. I'm gonna be a chippy.

Norma How a chippy?

Cooney It's whit Cooney men do.

Norma Just like that?

Cooney How do you mean?

Norma You just do it because it's what you do, do you?

Cooney Yeh. I suppose so.

Norma Oh.

Cooney Anyhow, the three biggest dudes ever were joiners.

Norma Who?

Cooney Han Solo, Jesus Christ and my Uncle Walter.

Norma Who's your Uncle Walter?

Cooney Watty Cooney? He's a Hell's Angel. He's got a big beard and a wooden sidecar.

Norma Will he give you an apprenticeship?

Cooney Aye, he says he will. He's got a boy on just now but so I've to stay at school till he's got a space.

Norma How long will that be?

Cooney Dunno. Boy he's got on just now isn't up to much. Might take a while to get their apprenticeship.

Norma Who's his boy?

Cooney Yvonne Lamont.

Norma He's got a girl for a boy? That's great. Modern for Stewarton.

Cooney He's from Kilmaurs.

Norma Even so.

Cooney And she isn't up to much.

Norma But it's still great. For women.

Cooney But she isn't up to much.

Norma How is Han Solo a joiner?

Cooney Harrison Ford was. How you getting aw Mystic Meg anyhow? You not working at Krazy Kutz any more?

Norma No. No, I am.

Cooney You wantin' to chuck it?

Norma It's just. It's. I'm. I got less Standard Grades than Rochelle McManus.

Cooney Rochelle's a right mongo.

Norma I know.

Cooney She got the bus to school.

Norma I know. That's the point.

Cooney And she got breast enlargements on the NHS cos her mum works in the chemist's and she said she was depressed.

Norma She got them cos she was self-harming.

Cooney You should go to college if you're that bothered.

Norma And then what?

Cooney Pff. You should just chuck it and get a giro.

Norma I suppose it doesn't matter anyway.

Cooney Naw. ~~Cos of the Muslims.~~
~~Muslim apocalypse aye? Aye.~~
Well at least you've left the school. That must be a relief.

Norma Honestly? It's just terrifying.

Cooney You'll be okay.

Norma But what is that?

Cooney How do you mean?

Norma What is okay? Really? I am okay. I'm no' poor or starving or homeless or sick or anything. I am okay. What does it do for me? Really? And I'm not even okay . . .

Cooney I know!

Norma What?

Cooney You should be a beautician.

She glares at him. He kisses her lightly.

Cos you're beautiful.

Norma D'you really like Jesus, Cooney?

Cooney Aye, man. Jesus is mint. He was aw hoors an' carry-oots and long hair. An' he pure died young. He's like Keith Moon.

Norma Who?

Cooney Aye, man.

Cooney notices the comic.

What's that?

Norma Em. A comic.

Cooney Let's see it.

Norma No.

Cooney How no?

Norma Em. Gonnae just don't, Cooney.

He takes it from her.

Cooney Come on, Norma – give up the juice. What's this? 'Gimp Man vs Super Ninja'.

Norma Don't. Please. Give me it back.

Cooney (*reads*) 'Gimp Man surveys Stewartopolis from the top of the Duck Building'
Stewartopolis? Comeontaefuck. No way. Seriously?

Norma Please, Neil.

Cooney Whose is it?

Norma No one's. Mines. It doesn't matter.

Cooney 'A T. J. McGuire Comic'? T. J. McGuire? No way! Gonky Trevor the sex-pest wrote this! He is one creepy wee weasel.

Norma Please, Cooney.

Cooney What does the J stand for? Jizz Janitor? Jobby Jabber?
Oh my God . . .

Norma Give it back.

Cooney NOM-RA? NOM-RA?

Norma What?

Cooney Look, Nom-Ra. Norma, that's you, man. You're Nom-ra, intit? You're 'Nom-Ra, mighty Princess of Pain'.

Norma takes the comic from him and looks.

Norma Em.
Looks like it.

He grabs it back.

Cooney Ginger Trevor pure wants into your scants, man.

Norma attempts to take the comic back from him. He kisses her on the lips. Reluctant at first she eventually kisses back.

Norma You're not very nice, Neil.

Cooney You love it.

Norma I don't . . .

He kisses her again.

. . . know why.

Cooney Cos I give you the sweet loving you need, baby. I'm super fly.

Norma Ha!

Michelle enters. She is crying.

What's wrong, Michelle? Michelle? What's wrong?

Michelle Sebastian.

Cooney Who's Sebastian? That's a gay name.

Norma She's her cat. What's happened to Sebastian?

Michelle She's . . . She's . . . She's . . .
She's got cancer.

She sobs.

Cooney Haw haw. Sebastian's got kitty-cancer.

Norma SHUT UP, NEIL!

Cooney 'S only a cat, man! Chill the fuck out.

Michelle Norma.

Norma He's going. You're going.

Cooney I'm going.

Norma I'll talk to you later. I'll text you.

Cooney leaves. Norma comforts Michelle until:

Michelle . . . It's the size of a tangerine. And because she's a cat that's like the size of a watermelon apparently. A big watermelon.

Norma God.

Michelle Yeh.

Silence.

Norma Are you going to need to put her down?

Michelle I can't do anything yet. Not until my mum's back.

Norma Have you told her?

Michelle No. It's better if I wait.

Norma Will you tell Minnie?

Michelle Don't know.

Norma You shouldnae be on your own in that house, Michelle. Come and stay at ours.

Michelle Hardly.

Norma Please? You're Barry's girlfriend.

Michelle Exactly. Your mum hates me. She near enough paid for Barry's whole trip to get him away from . . . sorry. Sorry. I didn't mean. Sorry.

Norma starts to cry.

I'm sorry, Norma. I'm just. I didn't. It's. I (really) don't *really* think she hates me . . .

Norma sobs.

Norma It isn't that.

Michelle It'll all be okay, Norma. Honestly. She's an old cat.

Norma It isn't that.

Michelle Minnie lived a full life . . .

Norma 'S not –

Michelle Barry'll be back soon. It's like the Wemyss Bay Buddhists say – all things are transitory . . . everything changes. Nothing is for ever.

Norma I know – that's what's wrong. Why do things ever need to change? Nothing gets any better, does it? Everything just gets worse and worse. I just want to press pause, Michelle, just for a minute. Catch my breath.
    I'm pregnant.

Michelle Oh. Right.

Sound of a train passing by.   sfx train
                                  lights down

SCENE FOUR

Lights up

Sunday.
    Cooney is texting. He sends and receives and chuckles to himself.
    He sings a chorus from 'I Know What Girls Like' by Jay-Z.
    His phone rings. ✳ sfx phone

What is it, Rochelle? I'm just texting you.

Pause.
    Cooney wanders downstage as he talks.

The now . . .

    . . .

I did.

Trevor enters. He attempts to pass behind Cooney without being noticed.

Rochelle, I texteed you.

    . . .

I'm getting the bus the now.

He sees Trevor.

Ho you, you fud.
Fucking stay away fae Norma.

He chases him offstage. lights down.

SCENE FIVE

Sunday, continued.
Rab is getting stripped for a swim. Michelle enters. She is more embarrassed by his partial nudity than he is.

Rab Awright.

Michelle Sorry. I didn't realise.

Rab What? There would be hunks in trunks?

Michelle No.

Rab You're here a lot.

Michelle I'm staying in my great-gran's house and it's . . . It's a bit . . . I mean it's nice to get a bit of fresh air. What's your excuse?

Rab I'm in training.

Michelle What for?

Rab That's the million-dollar question.

He stretches.

Michelle Enjoying the summer holidays?

Rab Em. Aye, I suppose I am aye. Aye. Break from the toil.

Michelle Do you miss it? Uni?

Rab No' really. How is your gran getting on?

Michelle I don't know. The same. Worse. It takes ages apparently.

Rab Oh.

Michelle Dying.

Rab Right, yeh.

Michelle She wants to go. She said. She says.

Rab What did she say?

Michelle 'I want to go.'

Rab And you're sure she meant dying? Sure she didn't mean like 'go home' or 'go out for a fag' or 'go on a wee trip to Saltcoats'?

Michelle Pretty sure. She keeps saying she's done – 'Oh Michelle, pet, I'm done.' Done done done.

Rab Yeh. That's awful.

Michelle Yes. No. I don't know. Maybe she's right. When I was there today. She. She.

Rab What?

Michelle She pooed herself.

Rab Eww that's minging . . . terrible, I mean terrible.

Michelle It's both. And because I was there, she didn't want to . . . she wanted to . . . she didn't say anything so I was just there talking to her about what was in the *Kilmarnock Standard* this week and about Mrs McGilp's hysterectomy and just normal stuff, and she looked like something had happened, like upset or ashamed or . . . I don't know, but she didn't say and so I just went on . . . jolly-jolly. I just kept going on and on and then I smelt it and there was a stain on her sheet and . . . forget it. Sorry.

Rab You can speak freely. No wire.

He pats himself down.

Michelle I know. I don't even want to talk about it – you know? What is there to say? Everybody dies always. And it's brutal. And the worst thing is it just makes you think about you getting old, and you dying yourself and how selfish is that?
God. I sound like a monster.

Rab No you don't. Come here.

He offers her a hug. She nestles in, then, feeling his naked torso against her skin, becomes self-conscious and pulls away.

Michelle *I'm fine.* Sorry. God.

Pause.

Rab I'm here but. You know. If you need –

Michelle I'm fine. Thanks.

Rab Well. If you ever want . . . Just if you . . . Anyway.

Michelle Thank you. Really. For listening.

Rab Anyway. Swimming . . .

Michelle Yeh, don't let me stop you.

Rab Oh. Right. Okay. Could you – would you mind, just keeping an eye on my clothes for me? Don't want any wee dicks running off wi' my scants, or, whatever.

Michelle Okay.

Rab Right then . . . See you.

She watches him as he runs up and barrels into the Ducky.
Norma enters. She plops herself at Michelle's feet.

Norma And actually, I mean in fact, what they actually don't tell you is . . . it's creepy.

Michelle Creepy?

Norma Some wee thing . . . growing in . . . living inside . . . in me. Like a parasite or a wee horrible living flump or like a wee pink leech or an alien or a tumour or . . . sorry. I didn't mean tumour . . .
But I've got squatters.

Michelle So what are you going to do? You know – *do*?

Norma I was thinking about writing to Britney. You know. Maybe she's got some clothes and stuff she doesn't need any more . . . or a pram . . . Shut up! What do you mean, what am I going to do?

Michelle Are you going to have an abortion?

Norma You mad? Who has abortions?

Michelle You're sixteen.

Norma So? It's Stewarton – you have the baby.

Michelle That's not true.

Norma Jenny Barr? Kelly Cock-handle? Sally Smith?

Michelle And?

Norma No one has abortions.

Michelle Yes they do. You just don't hear about it.

Norma I don't then.

Michelle Okay. You have time to decide.

Norma Maybe there's still a chance. Maybe I'm just late and the fourteen home tests were wrong and I'm just retaining water and –

Michelle Fourteen tests? *pause*

34

Norma I had to go to Kilmaurs to get them. Twice. I bought every pregnancy test in Kilmaurs twice.

Michelle Why did you have to get them in Kilmaurs?

Norma Has it been so long, Michelle? I would be as well telling my mum and dad myself if I bought them in the town. Get an advert out in the *Kilmarnock Standard* – 'NORMA GORDON PUTS OUT'. Except I forgot Peg McManus, Rochelle McManus's mum, works in the chemist's in Kilmaurs so . . .

Michelle Oh.

Norma Peg McManus is the media.

Michelle She might not say anything . . .

Norma Yeh, right – she's like the internet in a twin set.

Michelle Are you serious about Neil, Norma?

Norma Cooney?

She thinks about it.

Doesn't matter much now, does it?

Michelle Why? Don't you think he'd stick by you?

Norma He's sixteen. He can't commit to a brand of cider.

Michelle You need to tell him. Or your mum or dad. Or someone.

Norma No I do not. I'm not telling my mum, I'm not telling my dad and I'm certainly not telling Neil Cooney. I don't have to tell anyone. There is literally no one I can tell and I am going to tell literally no one. I am going to be one of those girls that never tell anyone and just wear baggy clothes and have it on the toilet after nine months.

Michelle Good plan.

Norma I can't think of a better one.

Michelle It's okay. It's going to be okay. It's all going to be okay.

Norma How can you say that? You of all people? Everything's fucked. It's all changed and it's still changing and nothing is ever ever going to be the same again.

Michelle Don't worry. You'll be fine. I promise.

Norma You can't promise that. I wish everyone would stop promising things they can't control . . .

Rab enters.

Rab!

Rab Haw haw – awright there, wee Norma? I'm back in full effect. Making summer in Stewarton Rabtacular. Give me some love.

Norma cheers up and hugs him.

Norma Eww, Rab, you're making me aw wet.

Rab Haw haw . . . some things never change.

Michelle God.

Rab I'm glad I ran into you anyhow, Norma. I wanted to talk to you about Trevor. You and Trevor are close, aren't you?

Norma No.

Rab No? You no' close now no?

Norma No.

Rab Oh.

Norma I mean. We're friends.

Rab Aye.

Trevor enters. He is exhausted from being chased around Stewarton by Cooney.

Awright, wee man . . . Trevor . . . What's wrong?

He puffs.

Trevor I've been getting chased –

He gasps.

– for about four hours.

He spits.

From Cooney.

Rab Who is this wee dweeb Cooney?

Trevor Ask Norma.

Norma He's just . . . He isn't . . .

Trevor He's her boyfriend.

Rab He's what? What are you doing? He's the sort of idiot that gives grebby wee dicks a bad name.

Michelle Rab . . .

Norma Neil isn't like that. He just seems dicky. He's sensitive. He's like a marshmallow dressed up like a Nazi.

Trevor No he's not! He's the dickest. He's like . . . licorice dressed like . . . Hitler . . . Space Hitler . . . Dinosaur Hitler.

Rab I'm afraid you're going to have to break up with him, Norma.

Norma I'm what?

Rab You cannae go wi' Cooney. Get him chucked.

Norma Are you joking?

Rab You're either with the McGuire boys or you're against them.

Norma *What?* If you think you can swan back into Stewarton and start telling me what to do with my life you are very much mistaken, Rab McGuire. I'll go out with who I like and the 'McGuire boys' can stick it.

Rab Are you listening, Norma?

Trevor Shut up!

Michelle Rab . . .

Rab Rab nothing. Do you hear me? I forbad it. In Barry's absence –

Norma Stick it!

Michelle Just *shut up*, Rab. For one second. Mind your own business.

Rab Michelle?

Norma exits. Michelle follows her.

Michelle Norma . . .

Rab Women ay?

Pause.

So. He spends all day chasing you around Stewarton? Like Wile E. Coyote? Meep meep!

Pause.

No playing. Man to man. What's going on?

Trevor What?

Rab You and Norma?

Trevor What?

Rab Don't gie's it. You look at her like you're a dog and she's the butcher's bins. What's going on?

Trevor Nothing.

Rab Really? Your slev says different.

Trevor Nothing!

Rab Exactly. Nothing. Nothing is right, Trevor. Some girls are just . . . theoretical – do you know what I mean?
   They get in your head and you think about them, relentless, but that's all that can ever happen. All that ever will happen.

Trevor You don't need to worry about me.

   Pause.

Rab There are these monkeys in South America. In the jungle, right? Daft wee monkeys. And the wee tribal dudes who live near hunt them – right? Are you listening?

Trevor Yes but –

Rab Shut up. So they're pure crazy on hunting these wee monkeys. They hunt them tae eat them – love eating them. Pure monkey-heid stew and aw guzzling roast-monkey-butt chunks, right – everything.
   Do you know how they hunt them?

Trevor I don't know.

Rab They get a vase. No' like Ming 'hing – just a basic, crude clay vase. They put an orange in the bottom and they tie it to a tree. Listening?

Trevor YES. Yes I'm listening.

Rab Right, so they leave these wee vases wi' the orange in the bottom lying about. Go for a relaxing restorative kip and then the next morning they get up and every vase has got a stupid wee monkey hinging oot it. Know how?

Trevor Mm.

Rab The monkeys grab a hold of the orange wi' their daft wee hauns and try tae pull them out except once they get a grip of the fruit they cannae . . .

He illustrates his story with mime.

Unless they let go of the orange – and they never dae, so the wee tribesmen guys, they just walk around gieing them a scone on the brew.

He particularly relishes miming clubbing the monkeys to death.

Do you see what I'm saying here, Trevor?

Trevor Monkeys are idiots?

Rab Aye, but you're a monkey. I'm a monkey. We're aw monkeys, man. Wee Norma's your vase. Let her go. You need to let go of the orange.

Trevor Is that it?

Rab Basically. Aye. It's just cos I care.

Trevor I care about Norma.

Rab As a friend . . .

Trevor *Uh-huh!*

Rab My Mexican pal Pepe –

Trevor Pepe?

Rab Aye, Pepe. Pepe has an expression. You ready?

Adopts thick Mexican accent.

'Thee hoh-nee, is not for thee dhon-kee.'

Trevor Give it a rest. I know. Okay? I know.

Rab What?

Trevor I know about you. I know all about you.
Let's both just mind our own business.

Rab What are you talking about?
Trevor.
Trevor! What are you talking about?

Trevor Your laptop password is Durrant.

Rab So? How do you know that?

Trevor I'm your wee brother.

Rab So?

Trevor I saw an email from College.

Rab That is a fucking liberty, Trevor.

Trevor I know. I'm sorry. What happened?

Rab Nothing.

Trevor I'm your brother.

Rab No. I'm *your* brother, Trevor. Nothing happened.
Don't say anything –

Trevor I won't! But what –

Rab The honey is not for the donkey.

Sound of a train passing by. ✕ sfx train
highlts down

SCENE SIX

Monday. highlts up
  Norma is waiting for Cooney. Michelle waits with her.

Norma Are your mum and her 'lover' back today?

Michelle God. 'Lover.' Shut up.

Norma Well?

41

Michelle Yeh. I hope they . . . It's been hard for . . . with the business and my nanna Minnie and everything.

Norma You get on wi' old Alice?

Michelle Yeh, I suppose. She's always been . . . I don't know . . . they're just my parents.

Norma How's Minnie?

Michelle Em. Not. You know.

Norma I was thinking of visiting her. I know you said no' to but . . . she always gave me sweeties.

Michelle I know. I'm not sure, Norma. It's grim. She isn't really there sometimes. She looks . . . old.

Norma Minnie's always been dead good to me. If it's my only. I mean, if she's going to . . . I mean. I just want to.

Michelle Maybe you shouldn't. Maybe it isn't. It might be better if.

Pause.

She would like to see you.

Norma Is she allowed grapes?

Michelle She can't really keep them down. She's got a mountain of them. They just get older and older and eventually the nurses take them away. It's like some kind of horrible fruity metaphor.

Norma Will I take her in a *My Weekly* or a *People's Friend* or something then?

Michelle If you like. I don't think she's reading. Maybe you could take her some flowers. She likes flowers.

Norma Okay.

Michelle You should prepare yourself, though. I mean. Really. She looks bad.

Norma Oh God, I need to pee again. Seriously, man, fuck being pregnant. I'm going to have to go behind the bushes.

Michelle Really?

Norma Really. Don't look.

She retreats behind a gorse bush.

Michelle What are you going to do about Neil?

Norma I don't know. Nothing.

Sound of Norma moving about behind the gorse bush.

Michelle You need to tell him.

Norma Tell him what? Ewww . . .

Michelle He has rights and responsibilities.

Norma We all do. Ew ew ew ew ew.

Michelle This is a bit weird.

Norma Yeh. You got any tissues?

Cooney enters.

Michelle HELLO, NEIL.

Cooney Aye. Hello.

Norma, having peed, is now trapped behind the bush.

You seen Norma Gordon?

Michelle Em. Yeh. She's here. She.

Cooney looks around.

Cooney Aye?

Michelle She must have . . . she'll be . . . she's about.

Cooney You alright, darlin'?

Michelle Yeh.

Cooney How's your pussy?

Michelle What?

Cooney Your cat? How's your cat?

Michelle She's being very brave, thank you.

Cooney Brave. Haw haw. My maw's man wis brave when he had the cancer. What's your options but intit? Even if you're pure bubbling and begging and aw that they still say you're brave. No' like the SAS but, is it? And she's a cat. Cat's urnae folk.

Norma emerges.

Norma Em. Hiya.

Cooney Were you in the bushes?

Norma Em. Aye.

Cooney How?

Pause.

Michelle She was looking for a contact lens.

Cooney A contact lens?

Norma Yeh.

Cooney You don't wear contacts.

Michelle I do. I lost it . . . but she was looking . . . because I can't see because I've lost a contact. I have contacts.

Cooney (*to Michelle*) I've got contacts too. Contacts in the UDA.

Michelle Oh well. I'd better be going.

Cooney Awright. Bye then, darlin'.

Michelle See you at the hospital, Norma.

Norma Yeh.

She exits.

Cooney At the hospital? How you going to the hospital, Norma? You got a wee check-up? A wee scan or something?

Norma No. I'm visiting her great-gran. How do you mean, 'wee scan'?

Cooney Were you having a slash in the bushes?

Norma Maybe.

Cooney Ewww you're pure boggin, man.

Norma I just had an emergency. You peed at a bus stop in broad daylight.

Cooney It's a man's world.

He kisses her forcefully. She pushes him away.

You're my best girl, int you? NORMA AND COONEY 4 IVA.

Norma What's going on, Neil?

Cooney You tell me.

Norma You're acting like a pure freak.

Cooney Nothing you want to tell me? No wee secrets? Surprises?

Norma . . .

Cooney It's alright, Norma. I know. I'm going to be a dad. I ken.

Norma How –

45

Cooney Never you mind how I ken, I just do.

Norma Oh God. I feel sick.

Cooney That'll be your ovaries. Don't worry. I'm going to stand by you. Just you and me.

Norma Listen, Cooney, Neil . . .

Cooney Me and my girlfriend.

Norma Neil. I'm so so sorry. I really didn't mean for . . .

Cooney Except of course we never did it, did we? Cos you're frigid – sorry, you've got fanny trouble intit? That right aye? So that must make it . . . an immasculate conception then, Norma? Is that it, aye?

Norma I'm sorry. I'm so sorry.

Trevor enters. He notices them only once, too late, then freezes.

Cooney Trevor! Why did you run away from me the other day, my man? I was just wanting to say hello.

Trevor Okay . . .

Cooney Hello!

Trevor Hello.

Cooney You know Norma din't you, Trevor?

Trevor Uh-huh.

Cooney 'Nom-Ra, Princess of Pain'. Zat it, aye?

Trevor's face falls.

And that would make you who – Gimp Man? That right? Or are you Super Ninja? It's difficult to tell – cos of the masks.

Norma I didn't show him. He just looked. I'm sorry, Trevor.

Cooney produces the comic. He starts to tear it slowly to pieces. With each rip Trevor becomes smaller.

Cooney Kinky, man, kinky. Anyway. Listen. I just wanted to say that if you want to draw up wee wank-fantasies aboot ma bird – that's totally cool, honestly. I wonder if you'll still want to after she's aw pure hefting beefy and pregnant but – you know, whatever . . .

Trevor Norma?

Cooney Cool. Listen babe. I need to get over to Kilmaurs now cos I'm nipping Rochelle – an' I huv been all along cos I'm a fucking baller. And she puts out like her muff is on fire. Why don't you just . . . I don't know? Trevor – do you want a go on some damaged goods?

Trevor launches himself in a frenzy at Cooney. Cooney easily knocks him to the ground and starts to kick him.

Norma Please. Please, Neil. I'm sorry. It isn't his fault. I'm sorry.

She gets in between them. Cooney considers pushing her aside but does not.

Cooney She thinks you are a pure joke, Trevor. She laughs at you.

Cooney spits as he exits.

Trevor (*to Norma*) You should just go too.

Norma I need to explain to you, Trevor.

Trevor It's fine. I get it. I'm not slow, Norma.

Norma I didn't show him. He took it.

Trevor I don't care. It doesn't matter. What do you see in him?

Norma Nothing. He's a tit.

47

Trevor What did you see in him?

Norma I don't know.

Trevor Can you just leave me alone?

Norma Don't you want to talk about anything?

Trevor What is it you want? You think you can just. When no one is. Whenever you. With Cooney's baby. No.

Norma It isn't like that.

Trevor I get it now, Norma. I'm not just waiting on a string. I'm not a lapdog. I'm not a monkey with his hand in a jar.

Norma You don't understand.

Trevor You think I'm just here. On hold. But I'm not. I have feelings too. I'm a real human person. I'm not just here to reflect the glory of you. The shining Norma light. I'm not some mirror that tells you how fantastic you are and makes you feel loved and wanted and special. I'm not here for comparison.

Norma I know. I'm sorry, Trevor. I know. I've been awful. I don't think you're . . . That's just Cooney – you know that's just Cooney?

Trevor I don't even care any more.

Norma Please, Trevor. You need to listen to me –

Trevor Did you even read the comic?

Pause.

No.

Norma Not yet . . . I mean . . .

Sound of a train passing by.

48

Act Two

SCENE ONE

Friday.
Rab and Michelle are dressed for a funeral.

Rab There'll be sausage rolls.

Michelle Tofu rolls.

Rab Tofu rolls? God. That's no kind of funeral. Soup, sausage roll and an Empire biscuit . . . dae yoose get an Empire biscuit aye? Or do yoose get like a Crypto Marxist Peoples' Co-operative Biscuit or some'hing? You cannae whack an Empire biscuit. With a biscuit that good it's a miracle we ever lost the Empire. Even old randy Gandhi couldnae passively resist an Empire biscuit.

Michelle Why are they called funerals? There's nothing fun about them. They should be called shiterals. I've been to four already and I've never been to a wedding. Or a christening. They're so depressing.

Rab What do you want? Dancing?

Michelle No. I don't know. Yes. No. Something, though. Something more than that horrible little crematorium beside the abattoir on the Irvine Road. It's like the inside of a ferry.

Rab Yeh.

Michelle And some disinterested minister and the wee rollers rolling the coffin off to oblivion. Oblivion kept neatly behind a stupid wee velvet curtain. Honestly – is that it?

49

Rab It's inevitable that any ceremony marking the passing of a life be anticlimactic. I mean, even if they had fireworks, a free bar and monkeys – that's still an unworthy, underwhelming conclusion to the miracle of existence.

Michelle Yeh.

Rab They'll have fuck-all to say at my funeral anyhow. May as well list my favourite TV shows – know what I mean?

He adopts the solemn voice of a Priest giving a eulogy.

'Robert Aloysious McGuire was a man who enjoyed the work of David Attenborough. Be it *Planet Earth*, *The Blue Planet* or (his favourite) *The Life of Mammals*, Rab was never happier than when lying prostrate on the couch, hands down his tracky bottoms inertly letting the goggle-box radiation wash over his pleasingly round coupon.'

She laughs. Encouraged, he continues.

'He also enjoyed *Match of the Day 2* (because Adrian Chiles isn't a cunt like Gary Lineker). And Jeff Stelling on *Soccer Saturday* – because he is indeed the don.'

Michelle is still laughing which encourages Rab to take the joke too far.

'But it wasn't all telly in Robert's life. In addition to watching TV he had an enduring lifelong love of porno which brung him much solace and spiritual fulfilment. Indeed he died wi' a stanner . . .'

He tails off, embarrassed. Rallying, he sings the funeral march.

Dum dum dee dum, dum dee dum dee dum dee dum.

He then changes to 'Angels' by Robbie Williams. His clowning wins her back round.

Michelle Stop it. Stop it, please. I shouldn't be laughing.
I shouldn't.

Rab Sorry.

Michelle No, it's actually nice.

Pause.

I wish I believed. I wish I did.
	In eternal life and heaven and flying vicars with magic
flutes and whatever else they believe in. God, the Buddha,
El Ron. I just wish I believed in something . . .

Rab Aye. Between you and me and the Ducky –
sometimes I wish I supported Celtic – you know, cos
they win mair and have a better history . . . and their fans
arnae Nazis but I inherently know they're wrong and
ahm right so . . . aw academic, intit?

Pause.

Em.
	So . . .
	You looking forward to Barry getting back aye?

Michelle No. I don't know. No. I mean. Where is he?
Why isn't he here?

Rab Did you ask him to come back?

Michelle Was I supposed to? Did I need to?

Rab No. I suppose . . .

Pause.

Michelle So this is it.

Pause.

I might contact *Watchdog*. Maybe Nicky Campbell could
get me satisfaction. How much worse can a spa holiday
go than dying during a treatment? The long weekended.

Fuck. My Aunt Alice was sixty. That isn't old. That isn't enough. Blood in her brain. What is that, Rab? How can that be?

Rab I don't know.

Michelle I was just getting to know her. Properly. I had all the time . . . I was awful to her, to them. Oh Rab, I was awful. We didn't get enough time. She didn't get enough time.

What happened?

Pause.

What's it like? Being dead?

Rab I don't know, do I?

Michelle You don't know? Rab McGuire, biggest boffin in East Ayrshire, is stumped? The best mind of our generation? Stewarton's great white hope –

Rab Stop.

Michelle Huge, pulsing brain –

Rab *Stop.* Seriously. Please. Don't.

Michelle Shy?

Rab No.

Michelle You shouldn't be.

Rab Yeh . . .

Pause.

We're aw governed by the laws of physics. It is a scientific fact that hearts and clocks slow down as they approach the speed of light – which is the point at which matter is converted to energy. Matter changes into energy – pure white light, the pure white light of creation. That's what has happened to Alice, Michelle. Though she's no longer round us – she's all around us.

He opens his arms like Jesus to illustrate his point.

Sorry. Physics . . . Gay.

Michelle No. But I mean . . .

Rab That's your eternal life.

Michelle Yeh.

Pause.

It's the shit kind of eternal life though. Like living on through your actions.

Rab Yeh.

Pause.

Michelle I thought about you, you know. When we all left school and you went off to Cambridge.

Rab You thought I was a wee ned.

Michelle I didn't. I knew you. You were like *Good Will Hunting*.

Rab *Bourne Ultimatum.*

Michelle What?

Rab You mean *Bourne Ultimatum*. I'm like *Bourne Ultimatum*. *Good Will Hunting*'s the one wi' the swotty janny.

Michelle I always imagined you at – God, this sounds stupid now I'm saying it – really sophisticated parties with intellectuals and rich people and everyone wearing black tie and . . . you know now I'm thinking about it – it's the Ferrero Rocher advert I'm picturing.

Is it like that?

Rab Not really.

Michelle But you do wear evening wear?

Rab Only in the evenings.

Michelle Naturally.
You look good in a suit.

Rab Thanks. I ken. Who doesn't look good in a suit but?

Michelle I really appreciate you coming with me.

Rab It's cool.

Michelle You're the only person I can talk to.

Rab Hey, it's cool. Honestly. 'Ain't no thing.'

They look into each other's eyes.
Pause.
He kisses her. Norma enters.

Norma What are you doing? Get your hands off her.

Rab It isn't how it looks.

Norma I've got a squint – I'm not blind!

Michelle I need to go. It's my Aunt Alice's funeral. I'm sorry.

Rab Wait. I'm coming.

Michelle No. Don't. Leave me alone.

She exits.

Norma Who even wants you here, Rab? Why are you back at all? Are there no girls in Cambridge no?
Barry's your pal.

Rab I know, but you don't understand.

Norma I understand what you were trying to do to her.

Rab 'Do to her'? I'm no' a rapist, Norma. Except, you know, by radical feminists' definition.

Norma She's Barry's girlfriend. You're his pal. He only went on holiday.

Rab This has nothing to do with you.

Norma It's got something to do with Barry but. She's griefstricken.

Rab I know.

Norma You're just a pure letch.

Rab That's no it. Her and Barry. That was at school. When you're sixteen – you don't have a clue, Norma.

Norma Yes you do.

Rab You don't. You don't know what you want. I wanted to marry Vera Iqbal when I was sixteen. Barry's away gallivanting –

Norma Travelling.

Rab And probably doing God knows –

Norma Helping the local poor children build a well.

Rab She doesn't need your teen-Taliban moralising. Today's . . .

Norma She's going to a funeral, isnae like prom, or the Oscars, she disnae need a date. Barry's meant to be your friend . . .

Rab Aye, we are. But we're pals more than friends. There's limits.

Norma You're completely unbelievable! Just leave her alone.

Rab I can't do that.

Norma She loves Barry.

Rab Where is he but? Where is he?

Norma Where are you going to be in a month's time? Back in Cambridge, so just leave her alone. You're not from here any more.

Rab Where am I from then? I'm just some brain that got away. But I don't belong there either, Norma. I'm like a fucking bisexual or something.

Norma Boo hoo. Why don't you tell Barry how lonely you are?

Cooney enters.

Cooney Gay suit.

Rab I've been looking for you.

Cooney Aye? I don't roll that way, mate. I'm straight. Ask Norma.

Norma Go away, Neil.

Rab Didn't I tell you to stay away from my brother?

Cooney You're just some swotty Wilbur, man.
What you going to do? Hit me with your dictionary? I should knock you out. You're old and fat, man.

He pats Rab on the stomach.

Rab COONEY!

Rab swats his hand. Cooney steps away.

Cooney Too many rich swan dinners?

Rab approaches Cooney with a strength of purpose that causes him to back away.

Oh aye, Cooney's pure scared.

He edges against the cliff with his back to the Ducky.

Ooo – I'm keeking my breeks.

He has gone as far as is possible.

What are you going to do now though? Fuck all. You're going to do fuck all cos you're just a snobby twonk.

*Rab sticks the head on him, causing him to drop
backwards into the Ducky.
Sound of a splash.*

Norma Rab – what have you done?

Rab looks over to check he's alright.

Rab ~~He's fine.~~
I'll see you later, Norma.

lights down

End of scene.

SCENE TWO

*A little while later. Norma is alone. Cooney enters. He is
muddy, dripping wet and draped in green plant life from
the Ducky. Norma suppresses her laughter. He looks
thoroughly pissed off as he trudges across the stage,
ignoring her, and exits.*

SCENE THREE

lights up.

Friday, later. Norma is alone. Michelle enters.

Norma Hi.

Michelle Hi.

Pause.

About before. Nothing happened. It wasn't . . .

Norma He's coming back, Michelle.

Pause.

You do love Barry don't you, though?

Michelle does not reply. Norma breaks the silence.

How was the funeral?

Michelle Shit.

Norma Suppose.

Pause.

I broke up with Cooney.

Michelle Maybe that's actually for the best.

Norma Yeh.

Michelle I mean. He can always see the baby.

Norma Yeh . . . Why would he see the baby?

Michelle Because he's the father?

Norma No, he isn't.

Michelle Oh. I thought.

Norma I know you did, but he isn't, so don't.

Michelle Thank God. He's a dick, Norma.

Norma I know.

Michelle Do you mind me asking . . .

Norma I don't know. He made me laugh. He's a tank. It's Stewarton. It's not exactly teeming with eligible bachelors. Full set of teeth and your own baseball cap and you're in the top twenty.

Michelle No. I mean. Do you mind me asking who is the –

Norma Yes, I do mind. I really mind. It was a mistake. Before I was even going with Cooney. I wouldn't have if I'd known. I didn't think it would have . . . should have . . . could have . . .

Michelle Immaculate conception?

Norma Ha.
It was a dishevelled conception, a shambolic conception
. . . a tragic conception.

Pause.

TREVOR. McGUIRE.
I know – right? Trevor McGuire. Trevor McGuire –
Trevor McGuire – Trevor McGuire.
The father of my pink shrimp is weird ginger Trevor
McGuire.

Pause.

Michelle Trevor isn't that bad . . .

Norma Not that bad? He's touched. It's an achievement
he can sit upright and use cutlery.

Michelle Why did you sleep with him?

Norma I don't have an answer to that question. Do you
know what I mean? There isn't an answer, one answer.
There's a million tiny little stupid answers.
I was lonely. It was cold. He kept saying funny things.
I felt fat. His hair was looking nice. No one else was out.
He reminded me of someone else . . . My mum and dad
are separated . . . I haven't seen my brother for months.
I've got a shit job . . . He really wanted to. I had a full
bottle of Kiwi Mad Dog. The sun set pretty. I'd never
done it before.

Michelle You'd never done it before?

Norma I know. What are the chances? Should have
bought a lottery ticket. Do you know the worst thing?

Michelle What?

Norma I like him.

*Trevor enters. Seeing Norma, he hesitates as though
about to turn round and flee.*

Don't. Please, Trevor. Don't. It's okay. Please.

Michelle I should . . .

Trevor I'm sorry about your mum's lesbian partner
dying, Michelle.

Michelle Thank you, Trevor. Anyway. I'm going to go.
I should be back at the purvey now anyway. See you
around.

Norma Bye.

She exits.

Trevor I was going to go for a swim.

Norma Really? You should. It looks okay. I've never seen
you . . . before, I mean. You don't really . . .

Trevor I can swim.

Norma No. I know. I know that. Of course you can.
Sorry. I just haven't seen you swimming up the Ducky.

Trevor No. I thought. It's a free country.

Norma Uh-huh. Absolutely. It is.

Trevor So . . .

Norma Sure, uh-huh. I mean. Go for it.

*Trevor begins to get undressed. He is evidently
embarrassed but continues as he feels he has a point
to prove.*

Trevor.

Trevor What?

Norma Nothing.

Norma But . . .

Trevor Mmm?

Norma I'm really sorry, I know you don't want to hear it and I know you must think I'm awful and maybe I have been awful, to you, I mean, no' maybe – I *have* been, but I really mean it, Trevor. Sorry. It's not just guilt or self-interest or whatever – I'm really, really sorry. Properly.

Trevor Whatever.

Norma No, though. Not 'whatever'. Not 'whatever' at all. It matters, Trevor. I know it does. I know I hurt you. I know.

Trevor You hurt me? You didn't even just hurt me, Norma. You took something from me. You took something I can never get back.

Norma I know.

Trevor I can't ever.

Norma I know that.

Trevor I wish I still was . . . Do you know? I wish I hadn't . . . I wish my . . . *virginity* could grow back.

Norma I know. I'm sorry.

Trevor Sorry's an ornament, Norma. It doesn't matter. It can't change anything. You can't change anything.

Norma I know that.

Pause.

It was my first time too, Trevor.

Trevor What do you want?

Norma produces 'Gimp Man vs Super Ninja', which she has painstakingly taped back together. It is almost more Sellotape than comic.

Norma It's beautiful, Trevor. Amazing. I mean. I think I got it back together right. The pieces weren't that small . . .

Trevor I know what you think of me. I've always known. But I know that you're wrong too. I know I'm ugly but –

Norma You're not ugly.

Trevor I know I'm ugly. I used to want to be handsome but I don't now because I am how I am. And I'm fine with it. And if I was handsome then maybe I would be horrible like Cooney. Like he is inside . . . And I'd rather be ugly.

Norma You're not ugly, Trevor. You need to listen to me.

Trevor Forget it. Just please never even talk to me again – alright? I just don't even want to –

Norma SHUT UP! God, Trevor. Just shut up. Alright? I'm having your baby, you stupid idiot!

Trevor Oh.

Pause.

Norma Going to say something?

Trevor Oh.

Pause.

Norma And before you ask – I'm sure.
I've never slept with anyone else.

Trevor Oh.

Norma And I'm not saying you have to be involved. You don't. I don't blame you. This wasn't your fault. I mean if you. Oh, Trevor . . .

He comforts her.

Trevor It's okay. It'll all be okay. Everything is going to be okay.

Norma Do you promise?

Trevor Yes. I promise.

They kiss. ~~Hug~~

Lights down [handwritten]

SCENE FOUR

Lights up – [handwritten]
dimmer [handwritten]

Friday, evening. Michelle is alone. Rab enters.

Michelle Hello there.

Rab Hi.

Michelle How are you?

Rab Me? I'm fine. How are you?

Michelle I'm okay.

Pause.

Rab I didn't come to the funeral. In the end. I thought. You know.

Michelle I'm sorry.

Rab You're sorry?

Michelle Yes. Rab, I didn't mean . . .

Rab I know. I wis . . . inappropriate.

Michelle Forget it. Seriously. It doesn't matter.

Rab You're grieving. And Barry's. I was out of line.

Michelle Norma's just a bit highly strung just now.

Rab You awright aye?

Michelle Yes. No. It's good to be in the fresh air. Away from the smell of flowers.

Rab Aye?

Michelle Popular lesbians receive a lot of flowers when they die. Our house is full of them. So is Corsehillbank Street. They smell bad enough now . . . all concentrated and floral . . . syrupy. It's like medicine. Imagine when they start dying too. Rotting flowers.

My mum didn't even say a word to me at the funeral. She's barely spoke to me since it happened.

Rab Now the funeral's over though . . . That's what it's for, intit? Draw a line in the sand.

Michelle She doesn't want to draw a line in the sand. She wants to go and drown herself in the ocean.

Rab Oh.

Michelle And my nanna Minnie's like the Terminator or something. She's a colour no human being should be, she's got tubes in every limb and she can barely speak and she just keeps on going. She's immortal. They're saying she's going to have to leave hospital soon but she can't look after herself and Sebastian's dead and no one's told her and . . .

I. Am. Completely. Numb.

Rab It'll get better. How can it get worse? I mean. Your . . .

He searches for the right words.

. . . mum's girlfriend has just died.

Michelle She was my . . .
It's like . . .
She's . . .
My Aunt Alice is dead.

Rab comforts her. They hold each other for a moment.
He lets her go, feeling self-conscious.
Pause.

So. Go on. Cambridge.

Rab What about it?

Michelle You tell me. What's it like?

Rab Fff.

Michelle Come on. I'm grieving. Bereft. Distract me.

Rab Oh God. There's nothing to say.

Michelle Tell me.

Rab So boring.

Michelle Tell me. You change the subject every time I mention it. It can't be that bad.

Rab I met a girl.

Michelle Oh.

Rab Julia. She was my gay-jakey pal Seb's sister. He had a wee thing for me. Natch.

Michelle Natch.

Rab I telt him the score but. Then he catches me continental kissing Julia an' he pure throws an eppy. He runs off to Morocco, drinks himself to death, and me and Julia break up.

Michelle God. Rab, I'm sorry.

Rab Then we both get married, her to the wealthy but gauche Canadian industrialist Rex Mottram. He's awfy gauche. But then so was I. Before Brideshead . . .

Michelle Be serious.

Pause.

Rab I've dropped out.

Michelle Why?

Rab School's easy. You can just . . . drift through.

Michelle You drifted six 'A's?

Rab Near enough.

Michelle I studied really hard and I got 'B's and 'C's.
Really hard. I drew mind maps and I took fish oil and
I hid notes in my pencil case . . . wrote on my arms . . .

Rab What am I meant to say? Good genetics . . . positive
beneficiary of cultural bias . . . wee bit of luck.
    You can't imagine what that place is like.

Michelle Amazing . . .

Rab It's in East Anglia.

Michelle It's * CAMBRIDGE *.

Rab Exactly. It's * CAMBRIDGE *.
    That isnae necessarily a good thing.

Michelle Explain why it's a bad thing. I don't believe you
found it too hard.

Rab Aw the folk at college are posh to the point of being
handicapped.

    Rab pulls a posh face.

It's no' just, like, folk fae up the Bowes Rigg Hill. They
aw went tae Eton and Harrow and Westminster. An' they
aw know each other. My room was sandwiched between
a Farquar – an' that's his Christian name – and a Jemima.
It's a cuntorium.

Michelle It can't be that bad.

Rab It is but. It is.

Pause.

But I still bottled it.

Michelle If you were unhappy. Life's short.

Rab Do you know much about football, Michelle?

Michelle I'm the only child of two lesbians. No.

Rab So I got signed on a YTS by Rangers. But 'many are called, few chosen', right? So for every Barry Ferguson (or whoever) who grinds the absolute best out his abilities, pure rinses it, and does justice to his talents an whatever, there's a dozen . . . hundreds . . . thousands of others. Waste themselves. There's tons of them in Scotland. It's the national disease. Fat bams who stuff their faces wi' pizza suppers and pissed-up pump dafties on a Saturday night. Guys who cannae step up to the plate and break the shackles of the steak-bake society an' they just . . . squander themselves. End up at Dundee United. I'm an Arab!

Pause.

I passed first year. I had a shit time but I passed. Then the first week of second, day by day, exponentially compounding, I felt like I was suffocating. It's a claustrophobic place. Then I had a lab on the Friday – this teacher guy – who was a wee gay PhD student himself, mind you, no' even a proper guy, ripped the piss out me in front of the whole class – about something I hud supposedly messed up in my lab . . . cos I'm the class clown, aye, fucking Rab the oik.

I wis just so sick of folk laughing at things I says that werenae funny. You know that way? Is it no' just the most patronising, demeaning, dehumanising, insufferable shittery? They were aw just laughing at me, Michelle.

And it was the straw that broke. I snapped. 'No more.'
I thought 'No more.' I just left . . . there and then, bailed.

Michelle You walked out?

Rab Aye. Aw they academics are smug idiots spend half
their time condescending and half their time leering at the
birds.

I stood up, says 'You are a supercilious wee cocktard,
mate, and I am jazzin'. And I walked out.

Michelle Wow.

Rab Then I get outside and down the street and I'm
buzzing. I go for a cigarette and realise I left my bag inside.

Michelle God.

Rab An' I wouldn't have minded, I mean who needs a
ring binder, Polypockets and Gaston and Spicer's
Introduction to Biodiversity? But it had my phone, my
wallet . . . and everything. So I go back, big breath, open
the door say – 'And another thing . . .'

Michelle And?

Rab I couldnae think of anything . . . at all. I just froze.

Michelle What did you do?

Rab After about a minute of just standing there . . .
All of them looking at me like total scum . . .
I shouts –
'Oppenheimer was shit at labs too and he invented the
atom bomb! MANHATTAN PROJECT, motherfucker.'
Then I just picks up my bag and leaves.

Michelle What do your mum and dad think?

Rab They think I finished second year so they're no awfy
up on the current state of my academic career.

Michelle What have you been doing?

Rab Working in a pub serving aw they chinless Henrys I couldnae stick at college. I wanted to come straight back but. My mum and dad are . . . Everyone is just . . .

There's a display board about me up at the school, you know . . .

Pause.

I'm back now though, Michelle. I'm back in Scotland and I'm not going anywhere. Just so you know. No holidays. No travelling. I'm here. Now. And I'm staying.

Just so you know.

Michelle Really?

Rab Really. Starting at Glasgow in September – you don't even need an interview, man.

Michelle I never seize the day.

Rab Oh?

Michelle My Aunt Alice was vegetarian and she exercised and she didn't smoke or drink really or anything and she died in a Monticelli mud-wrap at Crieff Hydro.

I'm going to die, Rab. So are you. So is Norma and Barry and Trevor and Dixon McGilp and *everyone*. And you don't know when. No one knows. You can't wait. We can't wait.

Pause.

Rab No . . .

Michelle You know what I felt like? During the funeral?

Rab What?

Michelle What I always feel like? At funerals?

Rab Em . . .

Michelle Horny. Isn't that funny?

Rab Hilarious.

Michelle So . . .

Rab Listen. Michelle. I don't want to take advantage . . .

Michelle You don't want to take advantage?

Rab Well. I mean.

Michelle I think I'm going for a dip. Do you fancy a dip, Rab?

Rab Emm. . . .

Michelle kisses him deep and long. She breaks away and begins to undress. He is dazed.

Michelle Well – are you planning on swimming in the Ducky like that?

Rab Aye . . . fuck it.

He runs up to the edge and dives in, fully clothed. Sound of a splash.
Michelle continues to get undressed in preparation for joining him. Just before she is naked, Norma enters with Trevor.

Norma What are you doing?

Michelle Nothing.

Norma I've told my mum, Michelle.

Michelle Great. I'm glad for you.

Norma Come on, Michelle, you've got to come with me.

Michelle What? Why?

Norma Barry's home!

Pause.

Your boyfriend? Barry? Barry's back. I emailed him when she died and he's come back. Come on! He's at the funeral looking for you.

Michelle looks at the edge of the cliff.
Lights.

lights down

SCENE FIVE

lights up

Rab McGuire enters. He is dressed for a funeral in a black suit and tie. He is soaking wet. His white shirt is muddy and his shoes leak water. He is exhausted. He looks around, sees he is alone, and opens his mouth to scream in frustrated anguish.

Rab ...

Lights.

lights down.

The End.